OH-SEW-SMALL
QUILTS

Oxmoor House ®

OH-SEW-SMALL QUILTS
©1995 by Oxmoor House, Inc.

Book Division of Southern Progress Corporation
P.O. Box 2463, Birmingham, AL 35201

Published by Oxmoor House, Inc., and
Leisure Arts, Inc.

Library of Congress Catalog Number 94-69239
ISBN: 0-8487-1263-3

Manufactured in the United States of America
First Printing 1995

Editor-in-Chief: Nancy J. Fitzpatrick
Editorial Director, Special Interest Publications:
 Ann H. Harvey
Senior Crafts Editor: Susan Ramey Cleveland
Senior Editor, Editorial Services: Olivia Kindig Wells
Art Director: James Boone

OH-SEW-SMALL QUILTS

Editor: Linda Baltzell Wright
Editorial Assistant: Laura A. Fredericks
Copy Editor: Jennifer K. Mathews
Production and Distribution Director: Phillip Lee
Production Manager: Gail H. Morris
Associate Production Manager: Theresa L. Beste
Production Assistant: Marianne Jordan
Senior Designer: Larry Hunter
Designer: Carol Loria
Illustrator: Kelly Davis
Publishing Systems Administrator: Rick Tucker
Photographer: Ryne Hazen

Contents

Dear Quilting Friends,

This is an invitation for you to enter the magical kingdom of little quilts. These miniature versions of their larger sisters make charming wall hangings, doll quilts, or framed pieces. Display them on tables, chests, mantels, and shelves in your own home or give them as gifts to friends and family.

Each of the ten small wonders in this book, all designed by the Vanessa-Ann Collection, has a charm and a personality all its own. Turn the pages to find ladybugs, blossoms, autumn leaves, hearts, trees, and more. There's sure to be one that touches your heart and inspires your fingers to sew.

You can create some of these miniature masterpieces in only a few days; others take a little longer. But all will become heirlooms that you'll cherish and display with pride for years to come.

Happy stitching,

WORKSHOP

Selecting Fabrics

The best fabric for quilts is 100% cotton. Yardage requirements are based on 44"-wide fabric and allow for shrinkage. All fabrics, including backing, should be machine-washed, dried, and pressed before cutting. Use warm water and detergent but not fabric softener.

Necessary Notions

- Scissors
- Rotary cutter and mat
- Acrylic rulers
- Template plastic
- Pencils for marking cutting lines
- Sewing needles
- Sewing thread
- Sewing machine
- Seam ripper
- Pins
- Iron and ironing board
- Quilting needles
- Thimble
- Hand quilting thread
- Machine quilting thread

Making Templates

A template is a duplication of a printed pattern, made from a sturdy material, which is traced onto fabric. Many regular shapes such as squares and triangles can be marked directly on the fabric with a ruler, but you need templates for other shapes. Some quiltmakers use templates for all shapes.

You can trace patterns directly onto template plastic. Or make a template by tracing a pattern onto graph paper and gluing the paper to posterboard or sandpaper. (Sandpaper will not slip on fabric.)

When a large pattern is given in two pieces, make one template for the complete piece.

Cut out the template on the marked line. It is important that a template be traced, marked, and cut accurately. If desired, punch out corner dots with a ⅛"-diameter hole punch **(Diagram 1)**.

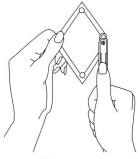

Diagram 1

Mark each template with its letter and grain line. Verify the template's accuracy, placing it over the printed pattern. Any discrepancy, however small, is multiplied many times as the quilt is assembled. Another way to check templates' accuracy is to make a test block before cutting more pieces.

Tracing Templates on Fabric

For hand piecing, templates should be cut to the finished size of the piece so seam lines can be marked on the fabric. Avoiding the selvage, place the template *facedown* on the *wrong* side of the fabric, aligning the template grain line with the straight grain. Hold the template firmly and trace around it. Repeat as needed, leaving ½" between tracings **(Diagram 2)**.

Diagram 2

For machine piecing, templates should include seam allowances. These templates are used in the same manner as for hand piecing, but you can mark the fabric using common lines for efficient cutting **(Diagram 3)**. Mark corners on fabric through holes in the template.

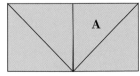

Diagram 3

For hand or machine piecing, use window templates to enhance accuracy by drawing and cutting out both cutting and sewing lines. The guidance of a drawn seam line is very useful for sewing set-in seams, when pivoting at a precise point is critical. Used on the right side of the fabric, window templates help you cut specific motifs with accuracy **(Diagram 4)**.

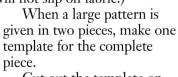

Diagram 4

For hand appliqué, templates should be made the finished size. Place templates *faceup* on the *right* side of the fabric. Position tracings at least ½" apart **(Diagram 5)**. Add a ¼" seam allowance around pieces when cutting.

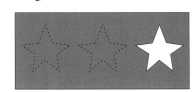

Diagram 5

Cutting

Grain Lines

Woven threads form the fabric's grain. Lengthwise grain, parallel to the selvages, has the least stretch; crosswise grain has a little more give.

Long strips such as borders should be cut lengthwise whenever possible and cut first to ensure that you have the necessary length. Usually, other pieces can be cut aligned with either grain.

Bias is the 45° diagonal line between the two grain directions. Bias has the most stretch and is used for curving strips such as flower stems. Bias is often preferred for binding.

Never use the selvage (finished edge). Selvage does not react to washing, drying, and pressing like the rest of the fabric and may pucker when the finished quilt is laundered.

Rotary Cutting

A rotary cutter, used with a protective mat and a ruler, takes getting used to but is very efficient for cutting strips, squares, and triangles. A rotary cutter is fast because you can measure and cut multiple layers with a single stroke, without templates or marking. It is also more accurate than cutting with scissors because fabrics remain flat and do not move during cutting.

Because the blade is very sharp, be sure to get a rotary cutter with a safety guard. Keep the guard in the safe position at all times, except when making a cut. *Always keep the cutter out of the reach of children.*

Use the cutter with a self-healing mat. A good mat for cutting strips is at least 23" wide.

1. Squaring the fabric is the first step in accurate cutting. Fold the fabric with selvages aligned. With the yardage to your right, align a small square ruler with the fold near the cut edge. Place a long ruler against the left side of the square **(Diagram 6)**. Keeping the long ruler in place, remove the square. Hold the ruler in place with your left hand as you cut, rolling the cutter *away from you* along the ruler's edge with a steady motion. You can move your left hand along the ruler as you cut, but do not change the position of the ruler. *Keep your fingers away from the ruler's edge when cutting.*

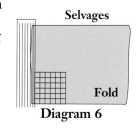

Selvages

Fold

Diagram 6

2. Open the fabric. If the cut was not accurately perpendicular to the fold, the edge will be V-shaped instead of straight **(Diagram 7)**. Correct the cut if necessary.

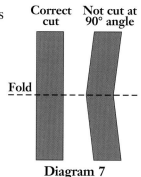

Correct cut — **Not cut at 90° angle**

Fold

Diagram 7

3. With a transparent ruler, you can measure and cut at the same time. Fold the fabric in half again, aligning the selvages with the fold, making four layers that line up perfectly along the cut edge. Project instructions designate the strip width needed. Position the ruler to measure the correct distance from the edge **(Diagram 8)** and cut. The blade will easily cut through all four layers. Check the strip to be sure the cut is straight. The strip length is the width of the fabric, approximately 43" to 44". Using the ruler again, trim selvages, cutting about ⅜" from each end.

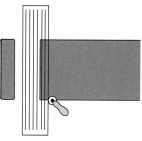

Diagram 8

4. To cut squares and rectangles from a strip, align the desired measurement on the ruler with the strip end and cut across the strip **(Diagram 9)**.

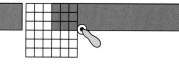

Diagram 9

5. Cut triangles from squares or rectangles. Cutting instructions often direct you to cut a square in half or in quarters diagonally to make right triangles, and this technique can apply to rectangles, too **(Diagram 10)**. The outside edges of the square or rectangle are on the straight of the grain, so triangle sides cut on the diagonal are bias.

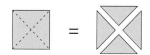

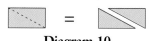

Diagram 10

6. Some projects in this book use a time-saving technique called strip piecing. With this method, strips are joined to make a pieced band. Cut across the seams of this band to cut preassembled units **(Diagram 11)**.

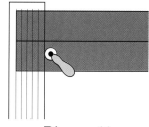

Diagram 11

Machine Piecing

Your sewing machine does not have to be a new, computerized model. A good straight stitch is all that's necessary, but it may be helpful to have a nice satin stitch for appliqué. Clean and oil your machine regularly, use good-quality thread, and replace needles frequently.

1. Patches for machine piecing are cut with the seam allowance included, but the sewing line is not usually marked. Therefore, a way to make a consistent ¼" seam is essential. Some presser feet have a right toe that is ¼" from the needle. Other machines have an adjustable needle that can be set for a ¼" seam. If your machine has neither feature, experiment to find how the fabric must be placed to make a ¼" seam. Mark this position on the presser foot or throat plate.

2. Use a stitch length that makes a strong seam but is not too difficult to remove with a seam ripper. The best setting is usually 10 to 12 stitches per inch.

3. Pin only when really necessary. If a straight seam is less than 4" and does not have to match an adjoining seam, pinning is not necessary.

4. When intersecting seams must align **(Diagram 12)**, match the units with right sides facing and push a pin through both seams at the seam line. Turn the pinned unit to the right side to check the alignment; then pin securely. As you sew, remove each pin just before the needle reaches it.

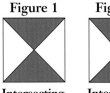

Figure 1 — Intersecting seams aligned

Figure 2 — Intersecting seams not aligned

Diagram 12

5. Block assembly diagrams are used throughout this book to show how pieces should be joined. Make small units first; then join them in rows and continue joining rows to finish the block **(Diagram 13)**. Blocks are joined in the same manner to complete the quilt top.

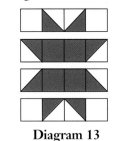

Diagram 13

6. Chain piecing saves time. Stack pieces to be sewn in pairs, with right sides facing. Join the first pair as usual. At the end of the seam, do not backstitch, cut the thread, or lift the presser foot. Just feed in the next pair of pieces—the machine will make a few stitches between pieces before the needle strikes the second piece of fabric. Continue sewing in this way until all pairs are joined. Stack the chain of pieces until you are ready to clip them apart **(Diagram 14).**

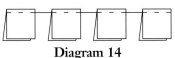

Diagram 14

7. Most seams are sewn straight across, from raw edge to raw edge. Since they will be crossed by other seams, they do not require backstitching to secure them.

8. When piecing diamonds or other angled seams, you may need to make set-in seams. For these, always mark the corner dots (shown on the patterns) on the fabric pieces. Stitch one side, starting at the outside edge and being careful not to sew beyond the dot into the seam allowance **(Diagram 15, Figure A)**. Backstitch. Align the other side of the piece as needed, with right sides facing. Sew from the dot to the outside edge **(Figure B)**.

9. Sewing curved seams requires extra care. First, mark the centers of both the convex (outward) and concave (inward) curves **(Diagram 16)**. Staystitch just inside the seam allowance of both pieces. Clip the concave piece to the stitching **(Figure A)**. With right sides facing and raw edges aligned, pin the two patches together at the center **(Figure B)** and at the left edge **(Figure C)**. Sew from edge to center, stopping frequently to check that the raw edges are aligned. Stop at the center with the needle down. Raise the presser foot and pin the pieces together from the center to the right edge. Lower the foot and continue to sew. Press seam allowances toward the concave curve **(Figure D)**.

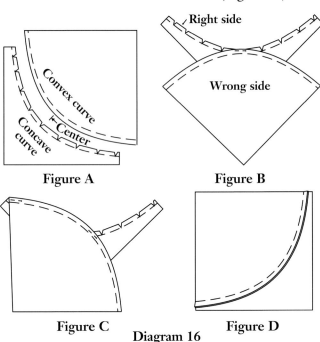

Figure A

Figure B

Figure C

Figure D

Diagram 16

Hand Piecing

Make a running stitch of 8 to 10 stitches per inch along the marked seam line on the wrong side of the fabric. Don't pull the fabric as you sew; let the pieces lie relaxed in your hand. Sew from seam line to seam line, not from edge to edge as in machine piecing.

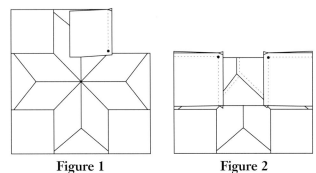

Figure 1

Figure 2

Diagram 15

When ending a line of stitching, backstitch over the last stitch and make a loop knot **(Diagram 17)**.

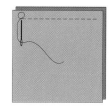

Diagram 17

Match seams and points accurately, pinning patches together before piecing. Align match points as described in Step 4 under Machine Piecing.

When joining units where several seams meet, do not sew over seam allowances; sew *through* them at the match point **(Diagram 18)**. When four or more seams meet, press the seam allowances in the same direction to reduce bulk **(Diagram 19)**.

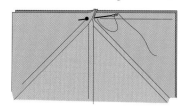
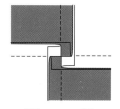

Diagram 18   **Diagram 19**

Pressing

Careful pressing is necessary for precise piecing. Press each seam as you go. Sliding the iron back and forth may push the seam out of shape. Use an up-and-down motion, lifting the iron from spot to spot. Press the seam flat on the wrong side. Open the piece and, on the right side, press both seam allowances to one side (usually toward the darker fabric). Pressing the seam open leaves tiny gaps through which batting may beard.

Appliqué

Traditional Hand Appliqué

Hand appliqué requires that you turn under a seam allowance around the shape to prevent frayed edges.

1. Trace around the template on the right side of the fabric. This line indicates where to turn the seam allowance. Cut each piece approximately ¼" outside the line.

2. For simple shapes, turn the edges by pressing the seam allowance to the back; complex shapes may require basting the seam allowance. Sharp points and strong curves are best appliquéd with freezer paper. Clip curves to make a smooth edge. With practice, you can work without pressing seam allowances, turning edges under with the needle as you sew.

3. Do not turn under any seam allowance that will be covered by another appliqué piece.

4. To stitch, use one strand of cotton-wrapped polyester sewing thread in a color that matches the appliqué. Use a slipstitch, but keep the stitch very small on the surface. Working from right to left (or left to right if you're left-handed), pull the needle through the

base fabric and catch only a few threads on the folded edge of the appliqué. Reinsert the needle into the base fabric, under the top thread on the appliqué edge to keep the thread from tangling **(Diagram 20)**.

5. An alternative to slipstitching is to work a decorative buttonhole stitch around each figure **(Diagram 21)**.

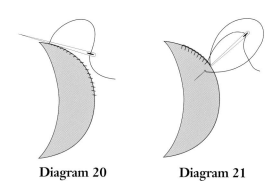

Diagram 20   **Diagram 21**

Freezer Paper Hand Appliqué

Supermarket freezer paper saves time because it eliminates the need for basting seam allowances.

1. Trace the template onto the *dull* side of the freezer paper and cut the paper on the marked line. *Note:* If a design is not symmetrical, turn the template over and trace a mirror image so the fabric piece won't be reversed when you cut it out.

2. Pin the freezer-paper shape, with its *shiny side* up, to the *wrong side* of the fabric. Following the paper shape and adding a scant ¼" seam allowance, cut out the fabric piece. Do not remove pins.

3. Using just the tip of a dry iron, press the seam allowance to the shiny side of the paper. Be careful not to touch the freezer paper with the iron.

4. Appliqué the piece to the background as in traditional appliqué. Trim the fabric from behind the shape, leaving ¼" seam allowances. Separate the freezer paper from the fabric with your fingernail and pull gently to remove it. If you prefer not to trim the background fabric, pull out the freezer paper before you complete stitching.

5. Sharp points require special attention. Turn the point down and press it **(Diagram 22, Figure A)**. Fold the seam allowance on one side over the point and press **(Figure B)**; then fold the other seam allowance over the point and press **(Figure C)**.

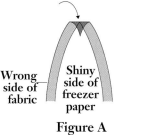

Wrong side of fabric   Shiny side of freezer paper

Figure A   **Figure B**   **Figure C**

Diagram 22

6. When pressing curved edges, clip sharp inward curves **(Diagram 23)**. If the shape doesn't curve smoothly, separate the paper from the fabric with your fingernail and try again.

Diagram 23

7. Remove the pins when all seam allowances have been pressed to the freezer paper. Position the prepared appliqué right side up on the background fabric. Press to adhere it to the background fabric.

Machine Appliqué

A machine-sewn satin stitch makes a neat edging. For machine appliqué, cut appliqué pieces without adding seam allowances.

Using fusible web to adhere pieces to the background adds a stiff extra layer to the appliqué and is not appropriate for some quilts. It is best used on small pieces, difficult fabrics, or for wall hangings and accessories in which added stiffness is acceptable. The web prevents fraying and shifting during appliqué.

Place tear-away stabilizer under the background fabric behind the appliqué. Machine-stitch the appliqué edges with a satin stitch or close-spaced zigzag **(Diagram 24)**. Test the stitch length and width on a sample first. Use an open-toed presser foot. Remove the stabilizer when appliqué is complete.

Diagram 24

Measuring Borders

Because seams may vary and fabrics may stretch a bit, opposite sides of your assembled quilt top may not be the same measurement. You can (and should) correct this when you add borders.

Measure the length of each side of the quilt. Trim the side border strips to match the *shorter* of the two sides. Join borders to the quilt as described below, easing the longer side of the quilt to fit the border. Join borders to the top and bottom edges in the same manner.

Straight Borders

Side borders are usually added first **(Diagram 25)**. With right sides facing and raw edges aligned, pin the center of one border strip to the center of one side of

Diagram 25

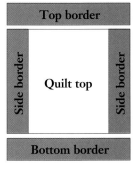

Diagram 26

the quilt top. Pin the border to the quilt at each end and then pin along the side as desired. Machine-stitch with the border strip on top. Press the seam allowance toward the border. Trim excess border fabric at each end. In the same manner, add the border to the opposite side and then the top and bottom borders **(Diagram 26)**.

Mitered Borders

1. Measure your quilt sides. Trim the side border strips to fit the shorter side *plus* the width of the border *plus* 2".

2. Center the measurement of the shorter side on one border strip, placing a pin at each end and at the center of the measurement.

3. With right sides facing and raw edges aligned, match the pins on the border strip to the center and corners of the longer side of the quilt. (Border fabric will extend beyond the corners.)

4. Start machine-stitching at the top pin, backstitching to lock the stitches. Continue to sew, easing the quilt between pins. Stop at the last pin and backstitch. Join remaining borders in the same manner. Press seam allowances toward borders.

5. With right sides facing, fold the quilt diagonally, aligning the raw edges of adjacent borders. Pin securely **(Diagram 27)**.

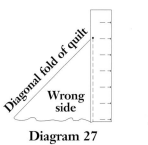

Diagram 27

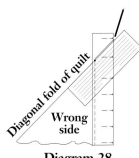

Diagram 28

6. Align a yardstick or quilter's ruler along the diagonal fold **(Diagram 28)**. Holding the ruler firmly, mark a line from the end of the border seam to the raw edge.

7. Start machine-stitching at the beginning of the marked line, backstitch, and then stitch on the line out to the raw edge.

8. Unfold the quilt to be sure that the corner lies flat. Correct the stitching if necessary. Trim the seam allowance to ¼".

9. Miter the remaining corners in the same manner. Press the corner seams open.

Quilting Without Marking

Some quilts can be quilted in-the-ditch (right along the seam line), outline-quilted (¼" from the seam line), or echo-quilted (lines of quilting rippling outward from the design like waves on a pond). These methods can be used without any marking at all. If you are machine quilting, simply use the edge of your presser foot and the seam line as a guide. If you are hand quilting, by the time you have pieced a quilt top, your eye will be practiced enough for you to produce straight, even quilting without the guidance of marked lines.

Marking Quilting Designs

Many quilters like to mark the entire top at one time, a practice that requires long-lasting markings. The most common tool for this purpose is a sharp **pencil**. However, most pencils are made with an oil-based graphite lead, which often will not wash out completely. Look for a high-quality artist's pencil marked "2H" or higher (the higher the number, the harder the lead, and the lighter the line it will make). Sharpen the pencil frequently to keep the line on the fabric thin and light. Or try a mechanical pencil with a 0.5-mm lead. It will maintain a fine line without sharpening.

While you are in the art supply store, get a **white plastic eraser** (brand name Magic Rub). This eraser, used by professional drafters and artists, will cleanly remove the carbon smudges left by pencil lead without fraying the fabric or leaving eraser crumbs.

Water- and **air-soluble marking pens** are convenient, but controversial, marking tools. Some quilters have found that the marks reappear, often up to several years later, while others have no problems with them.

Be sure to test these pens on each fabric you plan to mark and *follow package directions exactly*. Because the inks can be permanently set by heat, be very careful with a marked quilt. Do not leave it in your car on a hot day and never touch it with an iron until the marks have been removed. Plan to complete the quilting within a year after marking it with a water-soluble pen.

Air-soluble pens are best for marking small sections at a time. The marks disappear within 24 to 48 hours, but the ink remains in the fabric until it is washed. After the quilt is completed and before it is used, rinse it twice in clear, cool water, using no soap, detergent, or bleach. Let the quilt air-dry.

For dark fabrics, the cleanest marker you can use is a thin sliver of pure, white **soap**. Choose a soap that contains no creams, deodorants, dyes, or perfumes; these added ingredients may leave a residue on the fabric.

Other marking tools include **colored pencils** made specifically for marking fabric and **tailor's chalk** (available in powdered, stick, and traditional cake form). When using chalk, mark small sections of the quilt at a time because the chalk rubs off easily.

Quilting Stencils

Quilting patterns can be purchased as precut stencils. Simply lay these on your quilt top and mark the design through the cutout areas.

To make your own stencil of a printed quilting pattern, such as the one below, use a permanent marker to trace the design onto a blank sheet of template plastic. Then use a craft knife to cut out the design.

Quilting Stencil Pattern

Making a Quilt Backing

Some fabric and quilt shops sell 90" and 108" widths of 100% cotton fabric that are very practical for quilt backing. However, the instructions in this book always give backing yardage based on 44"-wide fabric.

When using 44"-wide fabric, all quilts wider than 41" will require a pieced backing. For quilts 41" to 80" wide, you will need an amount of fabric equal to two times the desired *length* of the unfinished backing. (The unfinished backing should be at least 3" larger on all sides than the quilt top.)

The simplest method of making a backing is to cut the fabric in half widthwise **(Diagram 29),** and then sew the two panels together lengthwise. This results in a backing with a vertical center seam. Press the seam allowances to one side.

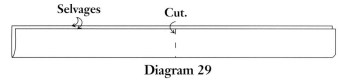

Diagram 29

Another method of seaming the backing results in two vertical seams and a center panel of fabric. This method is often preferred by quilt show judges. Begin by cutting the fabric in half widthwise. Open the two lengths and stack them, with right sides facing and selvages aligned. Stitch along *both* selvage edges to create a tube of fabric **(Diagram 30).** Cut down the center of the top layer of fabric only and open the fabric flat **(Diagram 31).** Press seam allowances to one side.

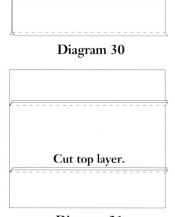

Diagram 30

Diagram 31

If the quilt is wider than 80", it is more economical to cut the fabric into three lengths that are the desired width of the backing. Join the three lengths so that the seams are horizontal to the quilt, rather than vertical. For this method, you'll need an amount of fabric equal to three times the *width* of the unfinished backing.

Fabric requirements in this book reflect the most economical method of seaming the backing fabric.

Layering and Basting

After the quilt top and backing are made, the next steps are layering and basting in preparation for quilting.

Prepare a large working surface to spread out the quilt—a large table, two tables pushed together, or the floor. Place the backing on the working surface wrong side up. Unfold the batting and place it on top of the backing, smoothing away any wrinkles or lumps.

Lay the quilt top wrong side down on top of the batting and backing. Make sure the edges of the backing and quilt top are parallel.

Knot a long strand of sewing thread and use a long (darning) needle for basting. Begin basting in the center of the quilt and baste out toward the edges. The basting stitches should cover an ample amount of the quilt so that the layers do not shift during quilting.

Machine quilters use nickel-plated safety pins for basting so there will be no basting threads to get caught on the presser foot. Safety pins, spaced approximately 4" apart, can be used by hand quilters, too.

Hand Quilting

Hand-quilted stitches should be evenly spaced, with the spaces between stitches about the same length as the stitches themselves. The *number* of stitches per inch is less important than the *uniformity* of the stitching. Don't worry if you take only five or six stitches per inch; just be consistent throughout the project.

Machine Quilting

For machine quilting, the backing and batting should be 3" larger all around than the quilt top, because the quilting process pushes the quilt top fabric outward. After quilting, trim the backing and batting to the same size as the quilt top.

Thread your bobbin with good-quality sewing thread (not quilting thread) in a color to match the backing. Use a top thread color to match the quilt top or use invisible nylon thread.

An even-feed or walking foot will feed all the quilt's layers through the machine at the same speed. It is possible to machine-quilt without this foot (by experimenting with tension and presser foot pressure), but it will be much easier *with* it. If you do not have this foot, get one from your sewing machine dealer.

Straight-Grain Binding

1. Mark the fabric in horizontal lines the width of the binding (**Diagram 32**).

A	width of binding	
B		A
C		B
D		C
E		D
F		E
		F

Diagram 32

2. With right sides facing, fold the fabric in half, offsetting drawn lines by matching letters and raw edges (**Diagram 33**). Stitch a ¼" seam.

3. Cut the binding in a continuous strip, starting with one end and following the marked lines around the tube. Press the strip in half lengthwise.

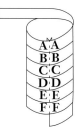

Diagram 33

Continuous Bias Binding

This technique can be used to make continuous bias for appliqué as well as for binding.

1. Cut a square of fabric in half diagonally to form two triangles. With right sides facing, join the triangles (**Diagram 34**). Press the seam allowance open.

Diagram 34

2. Mark parallel lines the desired width of the binding (**Diagram 35**), taking care not to stretch the bias. With right sides facing, align the raw edges (indicated as Seam 2). As you align the edges, offset one Seam 2 point past its natural matching point by one line. Stitch the seam; then press the seam allowance open.

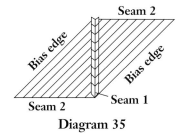

Diagram 35

3. Cut the binding in a continuous strip, starting with the protruding point and following the marked lines around the tube (**Diagram 36**). Press the strip in half lengthwise.

Diagram 36

Applying Binding

Binding is applied to the front of the quilt first. You may begin anywhere on the edge of the quilt except at the corner.

1. Matching raw edges, lay the binding on the quilt. Fold down the top corner of the binding at a 45° angle, align the raw edges, and pin (**Diagram 37**).

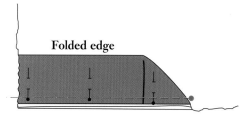

Diagram 37

2. Beginning at the folded end, machine-stitch the binding to the quilt. Stop stitching ¼" from the corner and backstitch. Fold the binding strip diagonally away from the quilt, making a 45° angle (**Diagram 38**).

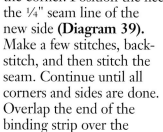

Diagram 38

3. Fold the binding strip straight down along the next side to be stitched, creating a pleat in the corner. Position the needle at the ¼" seam line of the new side (**Diagram 39**). Make a few stitches, backstitch, and then stitch the seam. Continue until all corners and sides are done. Overlap the end of the binding strip over the beginning fold and stitch about 2" beyond it. Trim any excess binding.

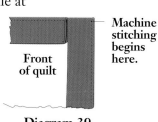

Diagram 39

4. Turn the binding over the raw edge of the quilt. Slipstitch it in place on the back, using thread that matches the binding. The fold at the beginning of the binding strip will create a neat, angled edge when it is folded to the back.

5. At each corner, fold the binding to form a miter (**Diagram 40**). Hand-stitch the miters closed if desired.

Diagram 40

Autumn Leaves

No two blocks are exactly alike in this tribute to fall. Although only simple piecing is involved, differences in color and positioning add a richness to the design and make the piecing challenging enough for experienced quilters.

Finished Quilt Size
18" x 27"

Number of Blocks and Finished Size
15 blocks   4" x 4"

Fabric Requirements

Yellow	⅛ yard
Tan	⅛ yard
Gold	⅛ yard
Cinnamon	⅛ yard
Rust	1¼ yards*
Burgundy	⅛ yard
Very light blue	⅛ yard
Light blue	⅛ yard
Medium blue	⅛ yard
Blue	⅛ yard
Dark blue	⅛ yard
Navy	⅜ yard
Backing	1 yard

*Includes 18" square for bias binding.

Other Materials
Gold, rust, and navy embroidery floss

Number to Cut**

Template A	4 yellow
	6 tan
	5 gold
	1 cinnamon
	6 rust
Template A rev.	2 tan
	4 gold
	2 cinnamon
	3 burgundy
Template B	2 yellow
	3 tan
	3 gold
	3 rust
	3 very light blue
	7 light blue
	7 medium blue
	9 blue
	4 dark blue
Template C	2 tan
	3 gold
	3 cinnamon
	3 burgundy
	4 very light blue
	6 light blue
	7 medium blue
	16 blue
	11 dark blue
Template D	2 light blue
	6 medium blue
	3 blue
	1 dark blue
Template E	1 very light blue
	2 light blue
	3 blue
	4 dark blue
Template F	2 very light blue
	4 light blue
	5 medium blue
	4 blue
	2 dark blue

**See Step 1 to cut borders before cutting other pieces.

Quilt Top Assembly

1. From rust, cut 2 (2" x 23") and 2 (2" x 30") strips for outer border. From navy, cut 2 (1" x 23") and 2 (1" x 30") strips for inner border. From navy, also cut 2 (1" x 23") strips for sashing. Set strips aside.

2. Join 1 dark blue C and 1 tan C along long edges to make 1 C/C square (**Leaf Block Assembly Diagram, Figure 1**). Join 1 yellow B to the square to make 1 B/C rectangle.

Join 1 blue C to 1 yellow A as shown (**Figure 2**). Join B/C rectangle to left edge of C/A rectangle to make a square.

Join 1 blue C to 1 yellow A as shown (**Figure 3**). Join C/A rectangle to right edge of square to make a large rectangle.

Join 1 blue C to 1 tan A as shown (**Figure 4**). Join 1 dark blue B to right edge of C/A unit to make a strip. Join strip to lower edge of large rectangle to complete leaf unit.

To complete the leaf block, join 1 blue E to right edge of leaf unit, as shown in **Quilt Assembly Diagram**. Join 1 dark blue F to lower edge.

Make 12 leaf blocks and 4 blue blocks, referring to **Quilt Assembly Diagram** for color and placement of pieces.

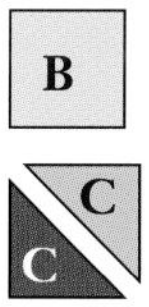

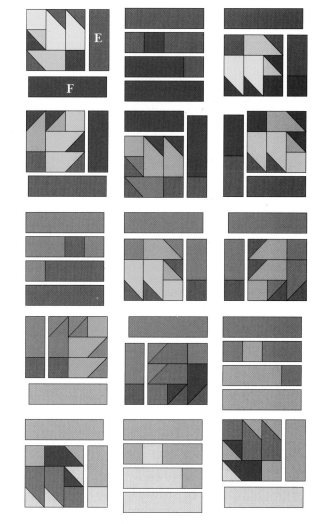

Figure 1

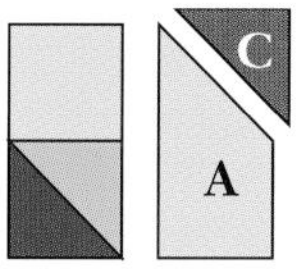

Figure 2

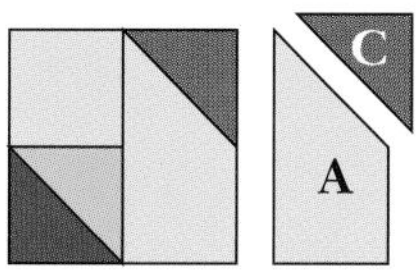

Figure 3

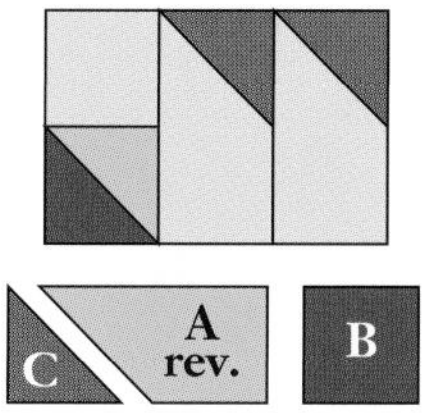

Figure 4

Leaf Block Assembly Diagram

Quilt Assembly Diagram

3. Arrange blocks in 3 vertical rows, as shown in **Quilt Assembly Diagram.** Cut 12 (1" x 4½") sashing strips from navy. Join 1 sashing strip to bottom edge of each of the top 4 blocks in each row. Stitch blocks together to make 3 vertical rows. Join rows with long navy sashing strips between.

4. Join navy inner border strips to rust outer border strips, matching lengths. Center and join long navy/rust strips to sides of quilt and shorter strips to top and bottom edges, mitering corners.

5. Referring to **Layout and Quilting Diagram,** mark placement for each stem. Outline-stitch with 2 strands of floss, using gold floss for yellow/tan and gold/cinnamon leaves and rust floss for rust/burgundy leaves.

Quilting

Mark horizontal lines ¼" apart on blue background. Mark ¼" inside edges of each leaf; then fill space with horizontal lines ¼" apart. Quilt using embroidery floss to match fabric color. Quilt the leaf pattern along border.

Finishing

Referring to instructions on page 11, make 2¾ yards of 2"-wide continuous bias binding from 18" square of rust fabric. Apply binding to quilt edges.

Layout and Quilting Diagram

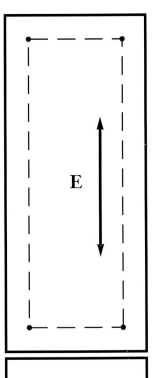

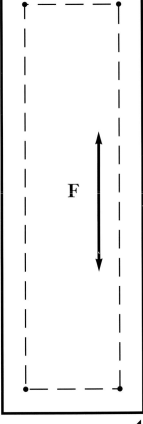

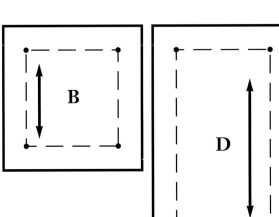

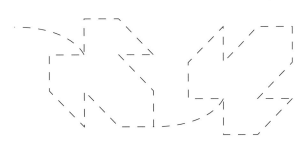

Leaf Quilting Pattern

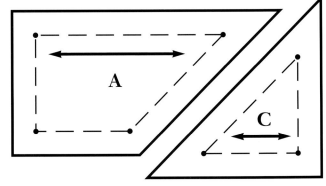

Ladybug

Gardeners welcome the sight of ladybugs in their gardens. And quilters will welcome these ladybugs with their easy-to-piece blocks and button spots.

Finished Quilt Size
33½" x 33½"

Number of Blocks and Finished Size
4 blocks   7" x 7"

Fabric Requirements
Red   ¼ yard
Black   ⅛ yard
Apricot   ⅝ yard
White   1 yard*
Gray   1 yard
Backing   1 yard

*Includes 18" square for bias binding.

Other Materials
Red quilting thread
Green embroidery floss
48 (⅜"-wide) flat black buttons

Number to Cut
Template A   32 red
Template B   64 apricot
Template C   48 apricot
Template D   16 black
Template E   32 apricot
                      68 white
Template F   4 white
Template G   4 white

Quilt Top Assembly
1. Follow **Ladybug Square Assembly Diagram** to make 16 Ladybug squares.

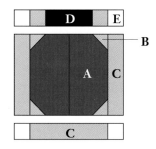

Ladybug Square Assembly Diagram

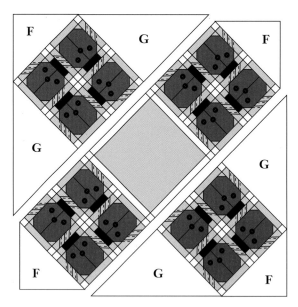

Quilt Center Assembly Diagram

2. Referring to **Ladybug Block Assembly Diagram,** join 4 ladybug squares, with the head of each ladybug facing the right side of the next ladybug. Repeat to make 4 blocks.

3. Transfer quilting lines (broken lines) and embroidery lines (solid lines) to strips (C) on right and left sides of each ladybug square. Backstitch with 2 strands of floss to embroider leg lines.

4. Cut 4 (1" x 6½") strips from white. Cut 1 (6½") square from apricot for center. Join 1" x 6½" white strips to right and left edges of 6½" apricot square. Join 1 white E to each end of remaining 1" x 6½" white strips. Join strips to top and bottom edges of square to complete center block.

5. Follow **Quilt Center Assembly Diagram** to assemble quilt center.

6. Cut 4 (7"-wide) border strips from gray. Referring to quilt photograph, center and stitch 1 gray border strip to each edge of quilt top. Miter corners.

Quilting
Mark remaining quilting lines, as shown in **Quilting Diagram.** Quilt on all marked lines with red thread. Also quilt ⅛" inside seams of ladybugs, in-the-ditch outside ladybugs, and along each seam of ladybug blocks.

Finishing
Referring to instructions on page 11, make 3¾ yards of 1½"-wide continuous bias binding from 18" square of white fabric. Apply binding to quilt edges. Referring to quilt photograph, sew 3 black buttons onto each ladybug, stitching through all layers.

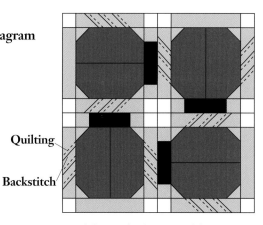

Quilting

Backstitch

Ladybug Block Assembly Diagram

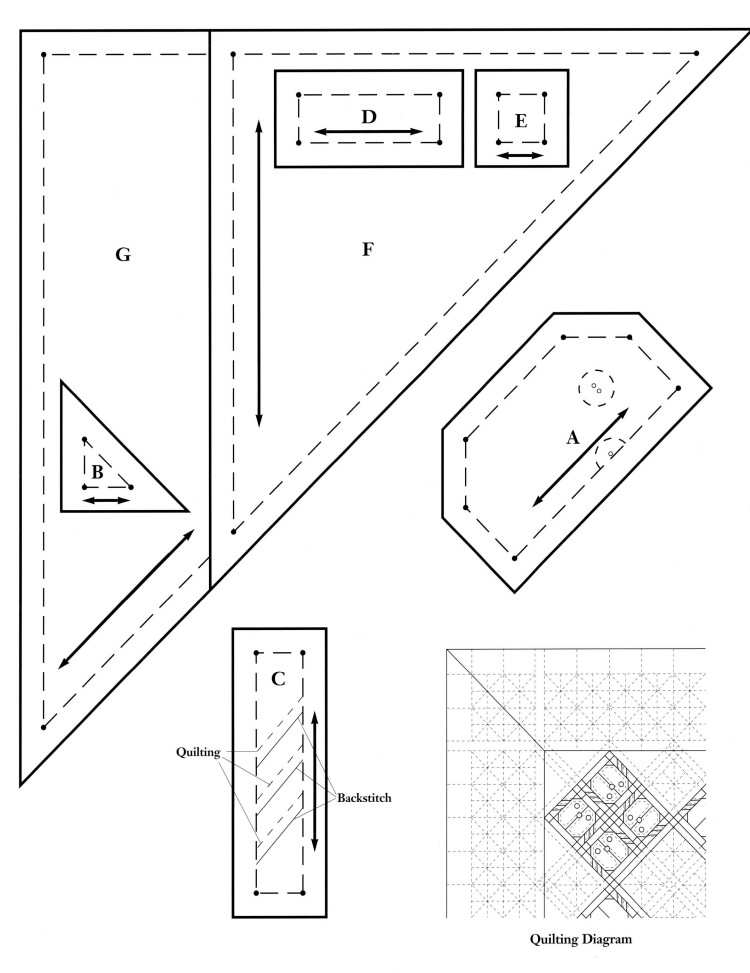

G

D

E

F

A

B

C

Quilting

Backstitch

Quilting Diagram

17

Fir Trees

Borrow a trick from Seminole patchwork to piece the small fir trees that give this quilt its charm. Join light and dark fabric strips, cut across the strips to make rows of checks, and then join the rows to make this precise grid of half-inch squares.

Finished Quilt Size

38" x 38"

Number of Blocks and Finished Size

9 blocks   8¼" x 8¼"

Fabric Requirements

Dark green print	¼ yard
Light green print	¼ yard
Light tan	¼ yard
Light brown	scraps
Rust stripe	⅞ yard
Light tan/rust pindot	⅜ yard
Blue-gray	scraps
Gray-green print	¼ yard
Light tan/navy pindot	¾ yard
Gold	1 yard*
Backing	1¼ yards

*Includes 18" square for bias binding.

Number to Cut

Template A	18 light tan
Template C	18 light tan
Template D	9 light brown
Template E	16 blue/gray
1"-wide strips	153" dark green print
	162" light green print
	72" light tan

Quilt Top Assembly

(*Note:* To prevent raveling, machine-stitch seams when using this technique.)

1. Cut 1 (1") square from 1 end of 1 light green strip for Row 1.

To make Row 2, cut 1 (9") length from both dark green print and light green print strips. Join strips along 1 long edge. Cut across band to make 1 (1"-wide) light/dark strip, as shown in **Strip Piecing Diagram, Figure 1.**

To make Row 3, repeat the joining and cutting process, using 2 light green print and 2 dark green print 9" strips (**Figure 2**).

Continue to piece and cut 9" strips to make rows 4–8, always alternating color, and referring to **Tree Block Assembly Diagram, Figure 1** for number and placement of strips.

2. Before joining, lay out all strips for first tree in rows, to be sure you have pieced them correctly. Join rows 1 and 2.

Cut 1 (1¾") length from light tan strip and join to the left edge of rows 1 and 2 (**Figure 2**). Join rows 3, 4, and 5 to rows 1 and 2, as shown in **Figure 3**. Cut 1 (3") length from light tan strip and join to left edge of joined strips (**Figure 4**).

Cut 1 (1¾") length from light tan strip and join to right edge of Row 7, as shown in **Figure 5**. Cut 1 (3") length and join to the right edge of Row 8. Join rows 6, 7, and 8 to rows 1–5 to complete piecing of tree.

Join 1 light tan A to each side of tree top, so that dots at corners of As meet intersection of seam allowance of dark green square at tree top (**Figure 6**).

3. Place Template B over pieced block, matching top and sides of template with top and sides of As. Mark outline of template on tree portion of block; then cut along outline to trim excess fabric from bottom and sides of tree shape.

4. Join light tan Cs to sides of 1 light brown D. Join C/D strip to lower edge of tree block (**Figure 7**). Repeat process to make 9 tree blocks.

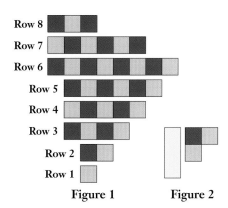

Figure 1 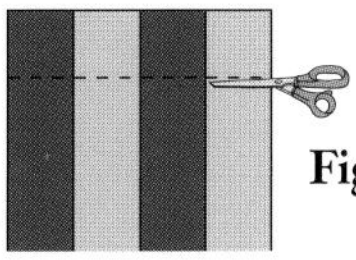   Figure 2

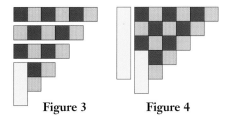

Figure 3   Figure 4

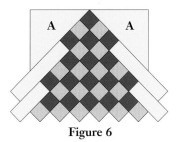

Figure 5

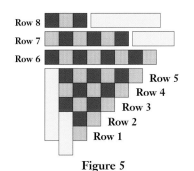

Figure 6

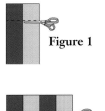

Figure 1

Figure 2

Strip Piecing Diagram

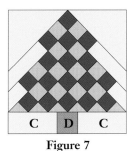

Figure 7

Tree Block Assembly Diagram

19

5. Cut 36 (2½" x 8¾") strips from rust stripe. Center and stitch 1 strip to each edge of each tree block, mitering corners, as shown in **Quilt Center Assembly Diagram.**

Cut 24 (1½" x 8¾") strips from light tan/rust pindot. Join 3 tree blocks and 4 light tan/rust pindot strips, alternating blocks and strips. Repeat to make 3 rows of blocks.

Join 4 blue-gray Es and 3 light tan/rust pindot strips, alternating Es with strips to make 1 row of sashing. Repeat to make 4 rows.

Join rows of blocks and rows of sashing as shown to complete the pieced center.

6. Cut 4 (1½" x 30") border strips from gray-green print. Join 1 strip to right and 1 to left edge of quilt top. Trim excess fabric. Repeat to join remaining gray-green print strips to top and bottom edges.

Cut 4 (3½" x 38") border strips from light tan/navy pindot. Stitch 1 strip to right and 1 to left edge of quilt top. Trim excess fabric. Repeat to join remaining light tan/navy pindot strips to the top and bottom edges.

Cut 2 (8⅝") squares from gold. Cut 1 square in half diagonally to make 2 triangles. Repeat for other square.

Fold under ¼" seam allowance on long edge of each triangle. Place triangles on corners of quilt top, as shown in **Quilt Assembly Diagram,** matching short edges of triangles to raw edges of quilt top. Appliqué long edge of each triangle to quilt top. Trim excess border fabric from behind corner triangles, leaving ¼" seam allowances.

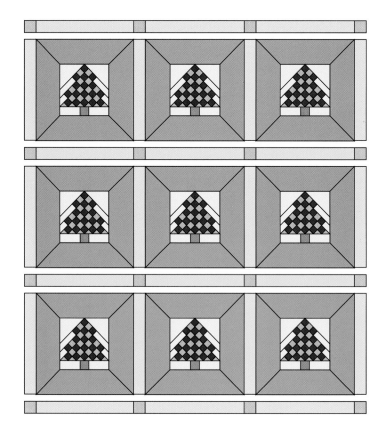

Quilt Center Assembly Diagram

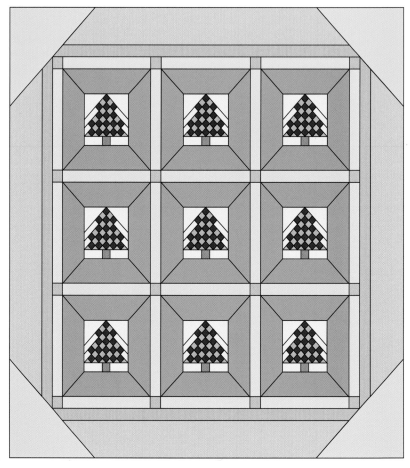

Quilt Assembly Diagram

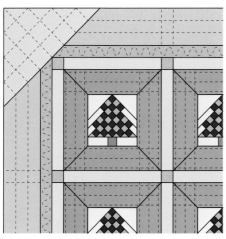

Quilting Diagram

Quilting

Referring to **Quilting Diagram,** mark 2 parallel lines on light tan/navy pindot border. Mark a diagonal grid of 1" squares in gold corner triangles. Mark quilting lines ¼" from seam lines on rust stripe borders of blocks and down center of border. Mark a wavy line on gray-green print border. Mark remaining lines as shown.

Quilt on all marked lines with tan thread. Also quilt in-the-ditch along seam lines of background of tree blocks, and along seam lines of borders and sashing. Quilt parallel lines ½" apart on tan at base of each tree.

Finishing

Referring to instructions on page 11, make 4½ yards of 2"-wide continuous bias binding from 18" square of gold fabric. Apply binding to quilt edges.

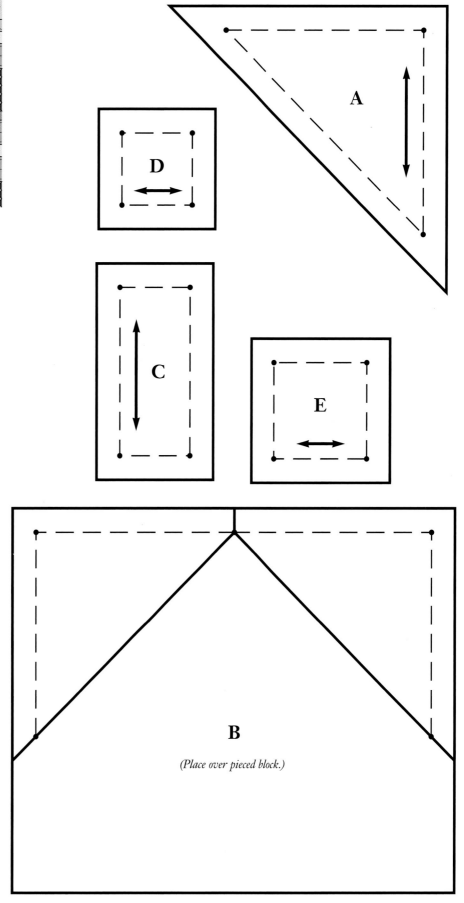

A

D

C

E

B

(Place over pieced block.)

Log Cabin Rose

Take a second look at our patchwork rose design, and
you'll discover that it's really an old friend, the log cabin
block, dressed up with some extra piecing within the strips.

Finished Quilt Size

26" x 26"

Number of Blocks and Finished Size

9 blocks   7" x 7"

Fabric Requirements

Red polished cotton	⅛ yard
White	⅝ yard
Gray-on-white stripe	¼ yard
Gray-on-white windowpane	⅛ yard
Light green	¼ yard
Dark green	⅛ yard
Gray print	1¼ yards*
Pink	⅜ yard
Backing	⅞ yard

*Includes 18" square for bias binding.

Other Materials

Gray quilting thread

Number to Cut**

Template A	36 gray-on-white stripe
	18 light green
	18 dark green
Template B	16 white
	20 pink
Red	1 (1¼" x 11¼")
	1 (1½" x 36")
White	1 (¾" x 11¼")
	1 (¾" x 13½")
Gray-on-white stripe	58½" (1¼"-wide)
Gray-on-white windowpane	1 (1½" x 13½")
	1 (1¼" x 11¼")
Gray print	(1¾" x 76½")
Light green	1 (1¾" x 15¾")

**See Step 1 to cut borders before cutting other pieces.

Quilt Top Assembly

1. From white, cut 4 (2¼" x 30") strips for outer borders. From light green, cut 4 (⅞" x 30") strips for inner borders. Set aside.

2. (*Note:* To prevent raveling, machine-stitch seams.) With right sides together, join 1¼" x 11¼" red strip and ¾" x 11¼" white strip along 1 long edge. Open up strip and press seam allowance toward red strip. Cutting across the band, cut 9 (1¼") segments. Sew remaining ¾"-wide white strip to left edge of 1 segment (**Rose Assembly Diagram, Figure 1**). Trim. Add 2 (1½"-wide) red strips to unit, using same stitch-and-cut method (**Figure 2**). Repeat to make 9 rose units.

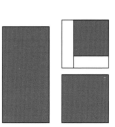

Figure 1

Figure 2

Rose Assembly Diagram

3. Join 1 stripe A and 1 light green A to make 1 stripe/light green A/A square. Repeat to make 18 squares. Join remaining stripe As to dark green As to make 18 stripe/dark green A/A squares.

Join 1 light green A/A square to 1 dark green A/A square to make 1 triangle strip as shown (**Leaf Assembly Diagram**). Repeat to make 9 strips. Make 9 triangle strips that are mirror images of the first set.

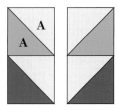

Leaf Assembly Diagram

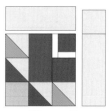

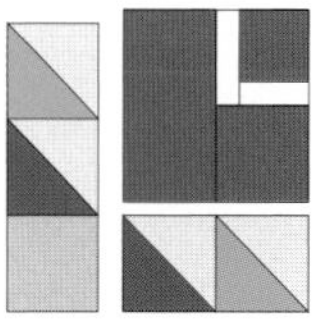

Figure 1   **Figure 2**

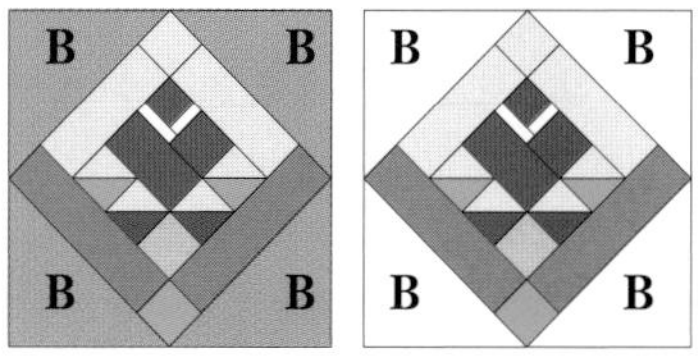

Figure 3

Block Assembly Diagram

4. Join 1 mirror-image triangle strip to lower edge of rose unit, as shown in **Block Assembly Diagram, Figure 1.** Repeat to join remaining mirror-image triangle strips to rose units.

Cut 1½"-wide windowpane fabric strip into 9 (1½") squares. Join 1 windowpane square to dark green triangle of each remaining triangle strip.

Join 1 strip to left edge of each rose unit, with green triangles to the outside.

5. Join 1 stripe strip to top edge of each square, as shown in **Figure 2.** Trim excess fabric. Cut 1¼"-wide windowpane strip into 9 (1¼") squares. Cut remaining 1¼"-wide stripe fabric into 3½" long strips. Sew 1 windowpane square to 1 end of each strip. Sew 1 stripe/windowpane strip to right edge of each unit, with windowpane square at top.

6. Join 1¾"-wide gray print strip to bottom edge of each square. Trim. Cut remaining gray print strip into 4¼" pieces. Cut 1¾"-wide light green strip into 1¾" squares. Add 1 square to 1 end of each gray print strip. Join 1 gray print/light green strip to left side of each unit, with green square at bottom.

7. Join 4 white Bs to sides of 1 block (**Figure 3**). Repeat to make 4 blocks. Join 4 pink Bs to sides of 1 block. Repeat for remaining blocks.

8. Join blocks together, alternating blocks with pink Bs and blocks with white Bs, as shown in **Quilt Top Assembly Diagram.**

9. Join light green border strips to white border strips. Join borders to quilt, mitering corners.

Quilting

Mark all quilting lines **(Quilting Diagram).**

Quilt with gray thread along seam lines of pieced center blocks on both sides of border, and on all marked quilting lines. (Do not quilt on seams that join pink and white triangles.)

Trim backing and batting to match quilt top.

Finishing

Referring to instructions on page 11, make 3 yards of 1¼"-wide continuous bias binding from 18" square of gray print fabric. Apply binding to quilt edges.

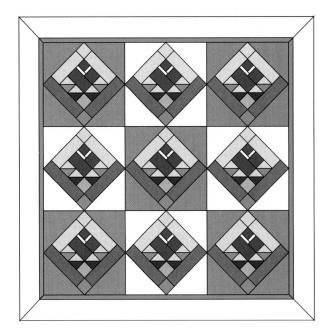

Quilt Top Assembly Diagram

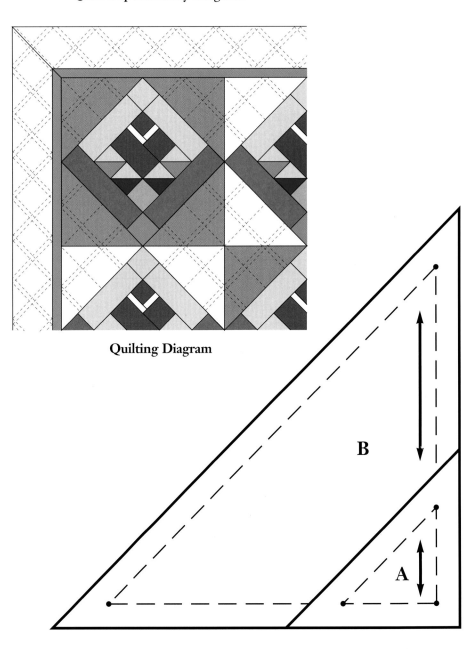

Quilting Diagram

In Full Bloom

Inspired by the radiant energy of summer, this quilt displays a clever combination of precision piecing and simple appliqué. Each appliquéd flower is actually a circle, pieced from colorful petal shapes and wedges.

Finished Quilt Size

40½" x 40½"

Fabric Requirements

Burgundy	¼ yard
Burgundy print	½ yard
Pink/burgundy print	⅜ yard
Pink/cream print	¼ yard
Rust	¼ yard
Dark green	1⅝ yard
Light green	⅛ yard
Small green print	⅛ yard
Large green print	⅛ yard
Cream/white print	2½ yards
Backing	1¼ yards

Number to Cut

Template A	12 burgundy
Template B	12 pink/burgundy print
Template C	12 cream/white
Template D	1 burgundy print
Template E	48 burgundy
	84 burgundy print
	84 pink/burgundy print
	36 pink/cream print
Template F	288 cream/white print
Template G	32 dark green
	17 light green
	18 small green print
	29 large green print
Template H	32 dark green
	36 cream/white print
Template I	4 dark green
Template J	3 burgundy
	9 burgundy print
	5 pink/cream print
	1 rust

Quilt Top Assembly

1. Join 1 burgundy A to 1 pink/burgundy print B. Repeat to make 12 A/B units. Add 1 cream/white print C to the right edge of each A/B unit **(Center Flower Assembly Diagram, Figure 1)**. Join A/B/C units to make a circle **(Figure 2)**. Join burgundy print D to center of circle. Set aside.

2. Join 1 pink/burgundy print E to 1 cream/white print F. Repeat to make 12 E/F units. Join units to make a circle **(Small Flower Assembly Diagram)**. Join 1 J to center of circle. Repeat to make 24 small flower blocks. Set aside.

3. Cut 1 (36½") square of cream/white print. Fold the square in half, horizontally and then vertically. Lightly mark the fold lines to divide quilt top into quarters. Mark diagonal lines from corner to corner of quilt **(Marking Quilt Top Diagram)**. Use a compass to center and draw a 6"-diameter circle on quilt top.

Mark 10" from center along each horizontal, vertical, and diagonal line. Center and draw a 4"-diameter circle on each mark (A).

Mark 15½" from center along each horizontal and vertical line. Center and draw a 4"-diameter circle on each mark (B). Divide each of these circles into quarters, showing divisions on outside of circle with dots. Mark arc lines on quilt by placing point of compass at each A and point of pencil on corresponding B.

Mark 1 (7¾") square in each corner of quilt as shown. Mark 4¾" from outside corner along each diagonal line. Center 1 (4") circle on each mark. Mark each inside square 2¾" from outside edge of quilt. Center 1 (4") circle on each mark.

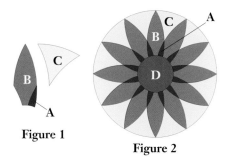

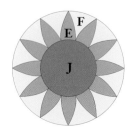

Figure 1

Figure 2

Center Flower Assembly Diagram

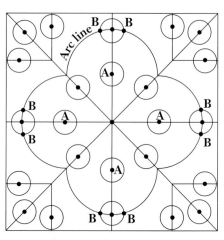

Small Flower Assembly Diagram

Marking Quilt Top Diagram

Quilt Top Assembly Diagram

Quilting Diagram

4. Cut 4½ yards of ⅞"-wide bias strips from dark green. From bias strips, cut 8 (3½"-long) pieces to use as stems. Center and appliqué strips over marked lines between large center flower and inner circle of small flowers **(Quilt Top Assembly Diagram)**.

Cut 8 (10½"-long) pieces from dark green bias strips. Center and appliqué over arc lines.

Cut 4 (8") and 8 (3½") lengths from dark green bias strips to make stems for flowers in corners of quilt. Appliqué short stems first, centering 3½" strips over lines; then appliqué 8" stems. Appliqué leaves as shown, noting leaf color placement.

5. Turn under seam allowance on center flower and small flowers and appliqué to quilt top, referring to **Quilt Top Assembly Diagram.** (*Note:* To make quilting easier, trim backing fabric from behind appliqués, leaving ¼" seam allowance.)

6. Referring to **Quilt Top Assembly Diagram,** join 9 cream/white print Hs with 8 dark green Hs, alternating colors. Repeat to make 4 border strips. Join strips to sides of quilt top. Join 1 dark green I to each corner of border.

Quilting

Mark quilting lines in the centers of flowers, in green H blocks of border, and in center of quilt, as shown in **Quilting Diagram.** Mark quilting lines ¼" inside seams on all white blocks. Also mark quilting lines ¼" outside appliquéd stems and leaves, inside leaves as shown, and outside flower petals. Mark ½" diagonal cross-hatching pattern to fill remaining space in border and background.

Quilt on all marked lines with cream thread. Also quilt in-the-ditch around the outside edge of the center flower and each small flower.

Finishing

Referring to instructions on page 11, make 5 yards of 2"-wide continuous bias binding from 18" square of dark green. Apply binding to quilt edges.

27

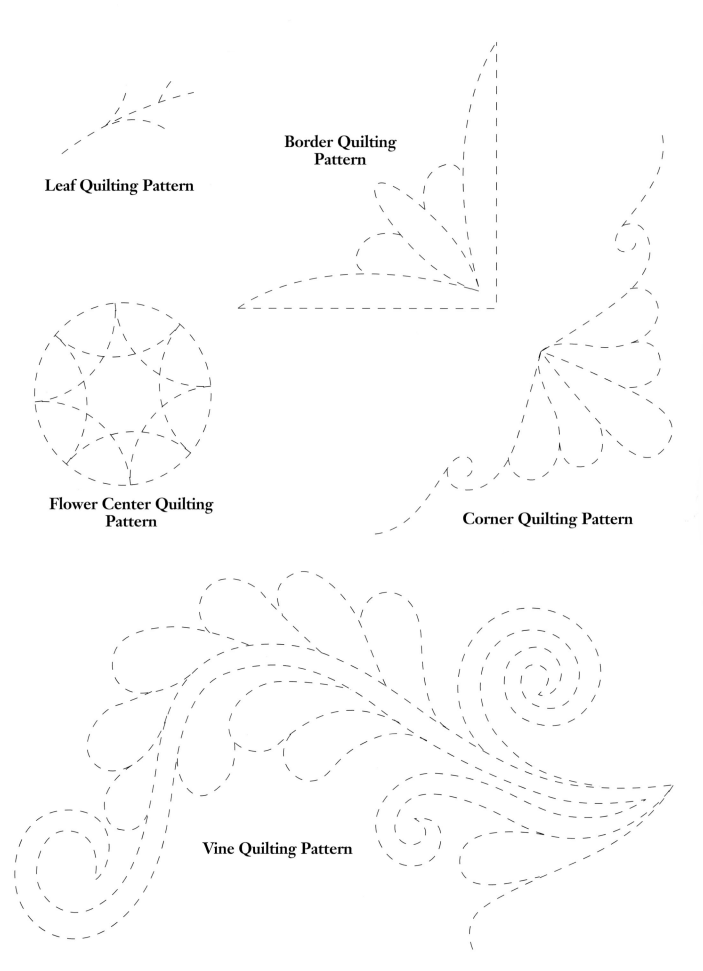

Leaf Quilting Pattern

Border Quilting Pattern

Flower Center Quilting Pattern

Corner Quilting Pattern

Vine Quilting Pattern

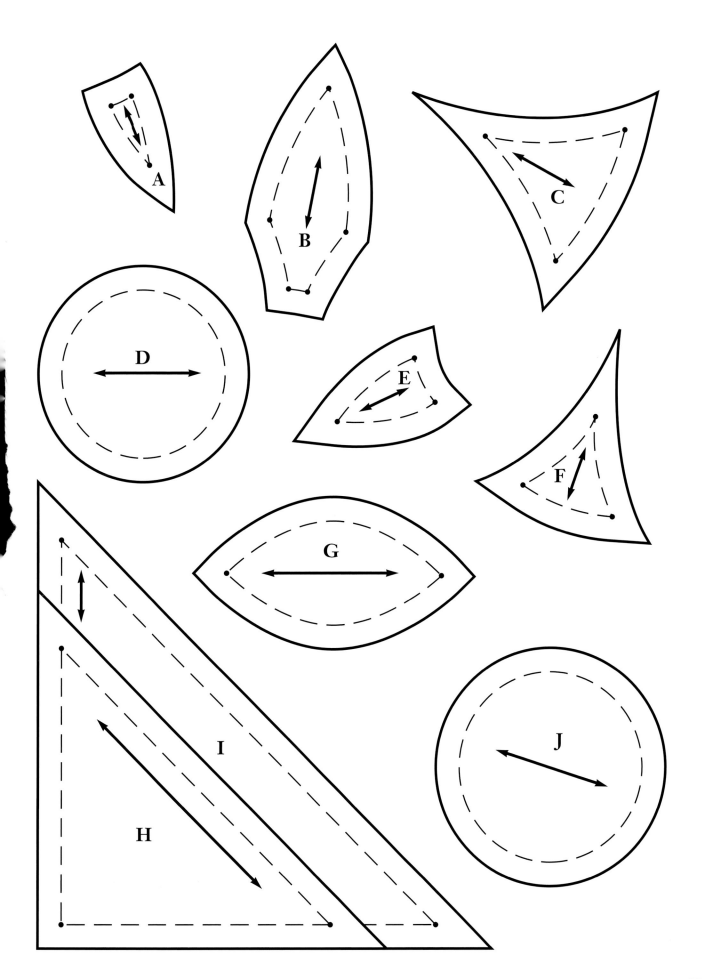

Clothesline

Many a mother has stitched scraps of her daughter's little dresses into a memory quilt that recalls favorite childhood moments. But if you can't bear to cut the dresses, display them on this clothesline instead. Pieced in brighter, bolder hues, the same design would make a fine showcase for a son's first tiny pair of jeans.

Finished Quilt Size

40" x 53"

Fabric Requirements

Pink print	¼ yard
Pink/blue pindot	½ yard
Pink	⅛ yard
Green	½ yard
White/green print	¼ yard
Muslin	½ yard
Pink/cream pindot	2 yards*
Green print	1¼ yards
Backing	1⅝ yards

*Includes 18" square for bias binding.

Other Materials

Green embroidery floss
1½ yards ⅜"-wide heavy white trim
6 to 8 pink ribbon rosettes
Baby clothing
5 (⅜") pink/white buttons

Number to Cut

Template A	30 pink print
Template B	15 pink/blue pindot
Template B rev.	15 pink/blue pindot
Template C	15 pink
Template D	15 pink/blue pindot
	2 muslin
Template E	10 green
	5 white/green print
Template F	5 pink print
Template F rev.	5 pink print
Template G	5 pink/blue pindot
Template G rev.	5 pink/blue pindot
Template H	5 pink
Template I	5 green
	5 muslin
Template I rev.	5 green
Template J	5 muslin
Template K	5 muslin
Template L	4 muslin
Template M	2 muslin
Template N	4 muslin

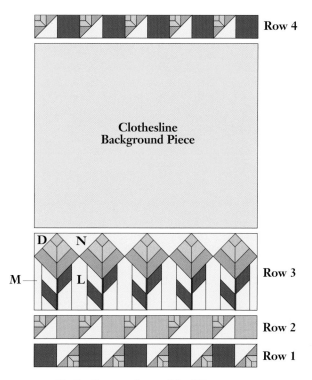

Quilt Center Assembly Diagram

Quilt Top Assembly

1. Join 1 pink print A to 1 pink/blue pindot B. Repeat with A and B rev. to make the mirror-image A/B rev. unit **(Flower Triangle Assembly Diagram, Figure 1).** Join units as shown.

Join 1 pink C to A/B unit to complete flower triangle. Stitch from corner dot to corner dot without catching B/B rev. seam allowances. Flip B/B rev. seam allowances out of the way, match the adjacent edge of C to B rev. edge, and join as before to complete the flower triangle. (You may find it easier to stitch this by hand.)

Repeat to make 15 flower triangles. Join each triangle to 1 D to make 15 small flower squares **(Figure 2).**

2. Join 1 green E to 1 small flower square **(Figure 3).** Repeat to make 5 flower rectangles. Join completed rectangles to make Row 1 of quilt, as shown in **Quilt Center Assembly Diagram.** Repeat to make second strip for Row 4.

In the same manner, join white/green print Es to remaining small flower squares. Join completed rectangles to make Row 2. Join rows 1 and 2.

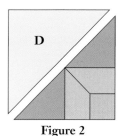
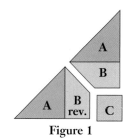

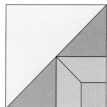

Figure 1   Figure 2   Figure 3

Flower Triangle Assembly Diagram

31

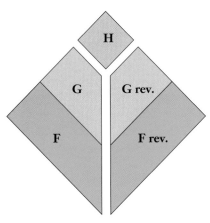

Large Flower Assembly Diagram

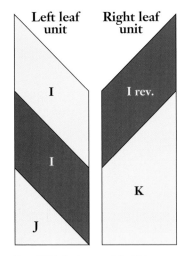

Leaf Unit Assembly Diagram

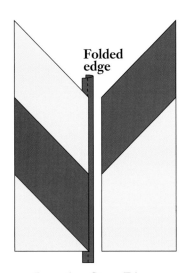

Inserting Stem Diagram

3. Join 1 pink print F to 1 pink/blue pindot G. Repeat with F rev. and G rev. to make F rev./G rev. unit **(Large Flower Assembly Diagram).** Join the 2 units as shown. Join 1 H to the unit to complete the large flower square. (You may find it easier to stitch H by hand.) Repeat to make 5 squares.

To make leaf units, join 1 muslin I to 1 green I. Referring to **Leaf Unit Assembly Diagram,** join 1 muslin J to I/I unit to complete left leaf unit. For right leaf unit, join 1 green I to 1 muslin K.

Cut 5 (1" x 5") strips from green for stems. Fold 1 green strip in half to make a ½"-wide stem; press. Pin strip to inside edge of right leaf unit, matching raw edges. Join left and right leaf units, as shown in **Inserting Stem Diagram.** Press folded edge to right. Turn piece over and trim ends of strip to match edges of leaf units.

To assemble Row 3, join 5 leaf units with 4 muslin Ls in between. Add 1 muslin M to each end of strip **(Quilt Center Assembly Diagram).** Join large flower squares to top edges of leaf strips. Add muslin Ns and Ds to fill in top edge of Row 3 as shown. Join Row 3 to Row 2.

Cut 1 (30½" x 24½") rectangle from pink/cream pindot. With right sides together, match 1 (30½") edge of rectangle to top edge of Row 3. Join. Join Row 4 to top edge of rectangle.

4. Cut 4 (5¼"-wide) border strips from green print. Stitch long strips to right and left edges of quilt top.

Cut 4 (5¼") squares from white/green print. Join 1 square to each end of 1 short border strip. Repeat to make second border strip. Join border strips to top and bottom edges of quilt top.

Quilting

Mark a diagonal line from upper left corner of clothesline section to center of far right N in Row 3, as shown in **Layout and Quilting Diagram.** Mark at ¾" intervals along top and left edges of pink/cream pindot rectangle. Draw vertical lines from the top edge to diagonal line. Draw horizontal lines from left edge to diagonal line. Mark parallel lines to fill in last 6" of rectangle beyond diagonal line.

In each white/green print corner block, mark echo-quilting lines ½" apart, ending with 1 (½"-long) horizontal line in the center. Quilt borders with 1½" diagonal cross-hatching pattern.

Quilt on all marked lines with cream thread. Also quilt in-the-ditch along all seams. Trim backing to match quilt top.

Finishing

Referring to instructions on page 11, make 5¼ yards of 2"-wide continuous bias binding from 18" square of pink/cream pindot. Apply binding to quilt edges.

Feather-stitch along seam where top meets binding, using 2 strands of green embroidery floss.

Position trim at top edge of pink/cream pindot rectangle as shown in quilt photograph. Tack in place with rosettes, allowing trim to hang loosely across the mid-section and allowing 10" extra length to hang free on each end. Fold ends as desired and tack. Place baby clothing along clothesline on quilt. Secure clothing by tacking rosettes through all layers. Sew 1 button in center of each H.

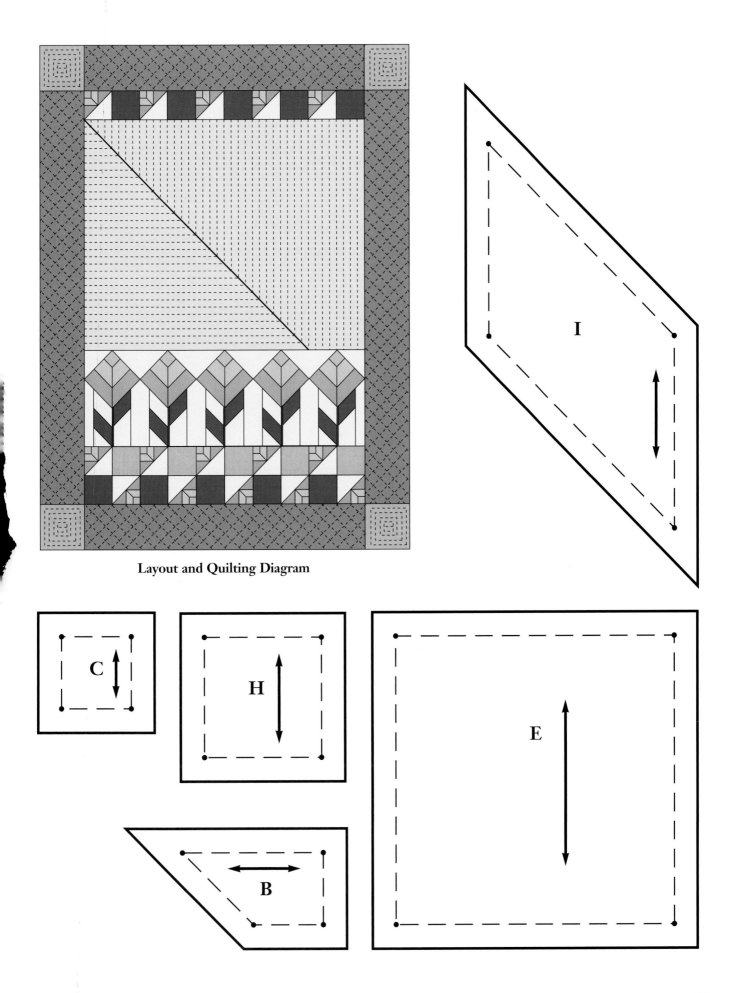

Layout and Quilting Diagram

I

C

H

B

E

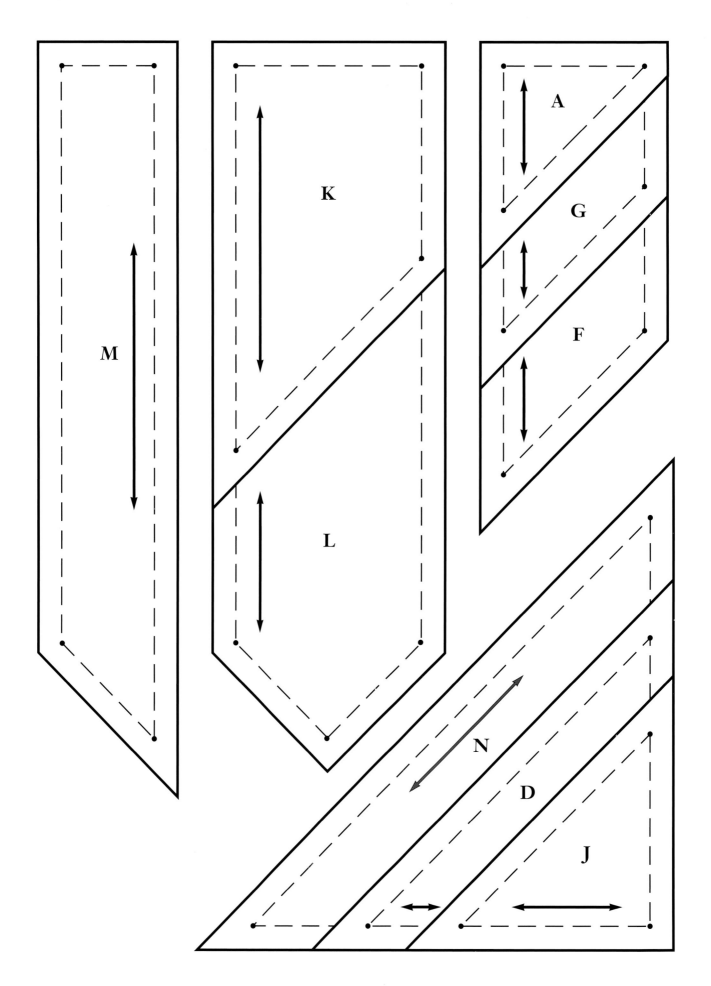

Springtime Stencil

To speed the construction of this picture-perfect quilt,
stencil springtime flowers instead of appliquéing them.
Each bouquet is framed in a stylized wreath pieced from
black and white triangles.

Finished Quilt Size

23¼" x 23¼"

Number of Blocks and Finished Size

9 stenciled blocks   3½" x 3½"
4 pieced blocks   3½" x 3½"

Fabric Requirements

White	⅜ yard
Black print	½ yard*
Backing	¾ yard

*Will need additional ½ yard if quilt is bound instead of framed.

Other Materials

Dark red, green paints
Stenciling supplies

Number to Cut**

Template A	4 white
Template B	60 white
	120 black print
Template C	9 white
Template D	24 white
Template E	8 white
Template F	4 white
White	9 (5") squares

**See Step 1 to cut borders before cutting other pieces.

Quilt Top Assembly

1. From black print, cut 2 (3½" x 20") and 2 (3½" x 25") strips for borders. Set aside.

2. Practice stenciling on scraps of white fabric, using small amounts of paint and a nearly dry brush. When satisfied with results, stencil design in center of each 5" block. Center Template C over design and trim each block to match template.

3. Join 1 white B and 1 black B along long edges to make 1 B/B square. Repeat to make 48 B/B squares. Join 1 black B to each white edge of each B/B square, as shown in **Pieced Block Assembly Diagram, Figure 1,** to make a B/B triangle. Repeat to make 24 B/B triangles.

Join long edge of 1 B/B triangle to 1 edge of 1 white A square. Repeat, joining 1 B/B triangle to each remaining edge of A to complete a square **(Figure 2)**. Repeat to make 4 A/B squares. Set aside remaining B/B triangles.

4. To make corner block, join 1 black B to 1 white edge of 1 B/B square. Join 1 white D to remaining white edge to make 1 B/D unit, as shown in **Corner Block Assembly Diagram, Figure 1.** Repeat, reversing color placement of B and D to make a mirror-image version of first B/D unit. Repeat to make 12 B/D units and 12 mirror-image B/D units.

Join B/D units to adjacent edges of 1 F, as shown in **Figure 2.** Repeat to make 4 B/D/F units.

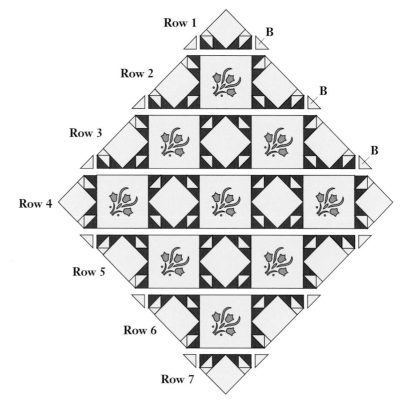

Quilt Assembly Diagram

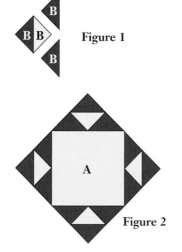

Pieced Block Assembly Diagram

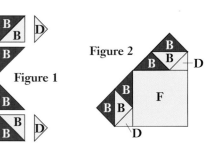

Corner Block Assembly Diagram

36

5. To make an edging block, join 1 B/B triangle and 2 B/D units to 1 E, as shown in **Edging Block Assembly Diagram.** Repeat to make 8 B/D/E units.

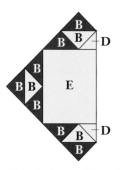

Edging Block Assembly Diagram

6. Join stenciled blocks, pieced whole blocks, edging blocks, and corner blocks, as shown in **Quilt Assembly Diagram.** Add white Bs as shown to complete each row. Join rows 1–7 to complete pieced center.

7. Join short black print border strips to top and bottom edges of quilt center. Join remaining border strips to quilt sides.

Quilting

Draw a diagonal line from corner to corner of each A, E, and F. Use white thread to quilt Xs. Also quilt close to outside edges of all white blocks and white triangles.

Tulip Stencil Pattern

Finishing

Frame with a black, 1½"-wide wooden frame. If you choose to bind your quilt instead of framing it, refer to instructions on page 11 to make 3 yards of 1½"-wide continuous bias binding from 18" square of black print fabric. Apply binding to quilt edges.

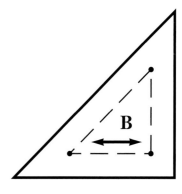

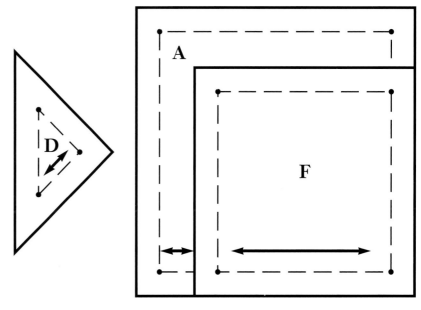

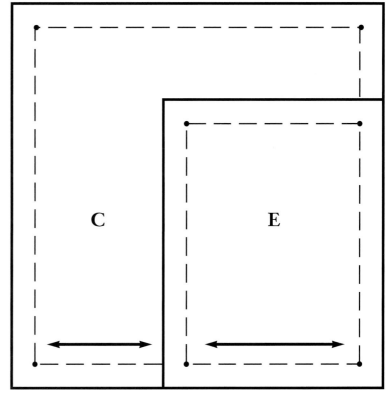

Gardener's Dream

Although the patchwork design may look difficult, this beautiful rose puzzle comes together like magic when you join the strips that make up each block. Just follow the row-by-row instructions and watch your garden grow.

Finished Quilt Size

34½" x 34½"

Number of Blocks and Finished Size

5 blocks   10" x 10"
4 pieced triangles

Fabric Requirements

Cream	¾ yard
Peach	¼ yard
Peach print	⅜ yard
Rose	⅛ yard
Green print	⅜ yard
Sage green	¼ yard
Dark green print	1¼ yards*
Backing	1⅛ yards

*Includes 18" square for bias binding.

Number to Cut

Template A	9 cream
Template B	5 cream
Template C	5 cream
	5 sage green
Template D	19 peach
	5 green print
Template E	40 cream
	5 green print
	18 sage green
Template F	19 peach
	19 peach print
	19 rose
Template G	5 cream
	5 green print
Template H	18 cream
	10 green print
Template I	10 cream
Template J	4 sage green
Template K	4 peach
Template L	16 green print
Template M	12 green print
Template M rev.	12 green print
Template N	16 dark green print
Template O	4 dark green print
Template P	4 dark green print
Template Q	4 cream
Template Q rev.	4 cream
Template R	8 sage green
Template S	4 cream
Template S rev.	4 cream
Template T	4 green print
Template U	4 green print

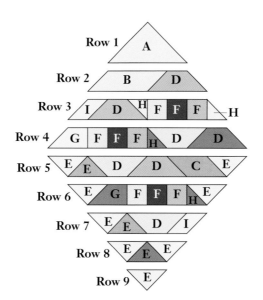

Block Assembly Diagram

Quilt Top Assembly

1. Each rose block contains 9 rows. Referring to **Block Assembly Diagram,** make rows as follows:

Row 1: Use 1 cream A.

Row 2: Join 1 cream B and 1 peach D.

Row 3: Join 1 cream I, 1 peach D, 1 cream H, 1 peach print F, 1 rose F, 1 peach F, and 1 cream H as shown.

Row 4: Join 1 cream G, 1 peach print F, 1 rose F, 1 peach F, 1 green print H, 1 peach print D, and 1 green print D.

Row 5: Join 1 cream E, 1 sage green E, 1 peach print D, 1 peach D, 1 sage green C, and 1 cream E.

Row 6: Join 1 cream E, 1 green print G, 1 peach print F, 1 rose F, 1 peach F, 1 green print H, and 1 cream E.

Row 7: Join 1 cream E, 1 sage green E, 1 peach print D, and 1 cream I.

Row 8: Join 1 cream E, 1 green print E, and 1 cream E.

Row 9: Use 1 cream E.

Join rows 1–9 as shown to make 1 peach rose block. Repeat to make 5 blocks.

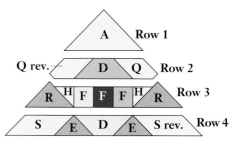

Triangle Assembly Diagram

2. Each rose triangle contains 4 rows. Referring to **Triangle Assembly Diagram,** make rows as follows:

Row 1: Use 1 cream A.

Row 2: Join 1 cream Q rev., 1 peach D, and 1 cream Q.

Row 3: Join 1 sage green R, 1 cream H, 1 peach print F, 1 rose F, 1 peach F, 1 cream H, 1 sage green R.

Row 4: Join 1 cream S, 1 sage green E, 1 peach print D, 1 sage green E, and 1 cream S rev.

Join rows 1–4 as shown to form a triangle. Repeat to make 4 triangles.

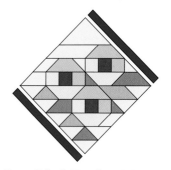

Rose Block Borders Diagram

3. Cut 8 (1¼" x 10") dark green print strips. Join strips to opposite edges of 1 rose block, as shown in **Rose Block Borders Diagram.** Repeat to make 4 blocks. Place remaining rose block between 2 dark green print-edged blocks and join to make 1 strip. Join 2

Quilt Center Assembly Diagram

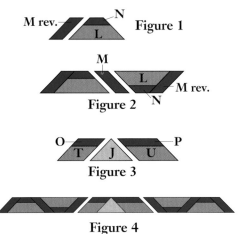

M rev.   N   Figure 1
L

M
L
   M rev.
N
Figure 2

O   T   J   U   P
Figure 3

Figure 4

Border Assembly Diagram

J

Layout and Quilting Diagram

peach print Ks to ends of strip **(Quilt Center Assembly Diagram)** to complete center band of quilt top.

Cut 2 (1¼" x 12") dark green print strips. Join 1 strip to long edge of 1 remaining K. Join dark green print-edged K and 2 rose triangles to 1 dark green print-edged rose square, as shown in **Quilt Center Assembly Diagram,** to make a large triangle. Repeat to make a second triangle that is a mirror image of the first.

Cut 2 (1¼" x 32½") dark green print strips. Place strips between the center band and the large triangles. Join to complete quilt top. Trim ends of strips to match edges of quilt.

4. Join 1 dark green print N to 1 green print L, as shown in **Border Assembly Diagram, Figure 1.** Join 1 dark green print M rev. to the left edge of the N/L unit. Repeat to make 4 M/N/L units.

Join 2 M/N/L units with 1 dark green print M to make left end of border strip **(Figure 2).** Repeat to make a second unit that is a mirror image of the first.

Join 1 dark green print O to 1 green print T, as shown in **Figure 3.** Join 1 dark green print P to 1 green print U. Join O/T unit and P/U unit to opposite edges of 1 sage green J to complete center unit of border strip.

To complete border strip, join border strips to center **(Figure 4).** Repeat to make 4 borders.

5. Match point of J on 1 border strip to lower left corner of rose D at bottom edge of quilt top **(Layout and Quilting Diagram).** Join the border strip to the quilt top. Repeat with 3 additional border strips. Join corners.

Quilting

Mark quilting lines in each peach print K. Draw a line from the outside corner of the triangle to the center of the long edge. Mark parallel lines 1" apart, as shown in **Layout and Quilting Diagram.**

Quilt in-the-ditch with cream thread around the center square of each rose, around the outside of each rose, and on all remaining seams. Quilt along marked lines in corner triangles. Trim edges of backing and batting to match top.

Finishing

Referring to instructions on page 11, make 4 yards of 1½"-wide continuous bias binding from 18" square of dark green print fabric. Apply binding to quilt edges.

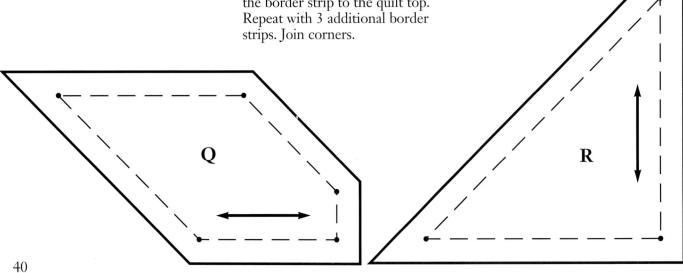

Q

R

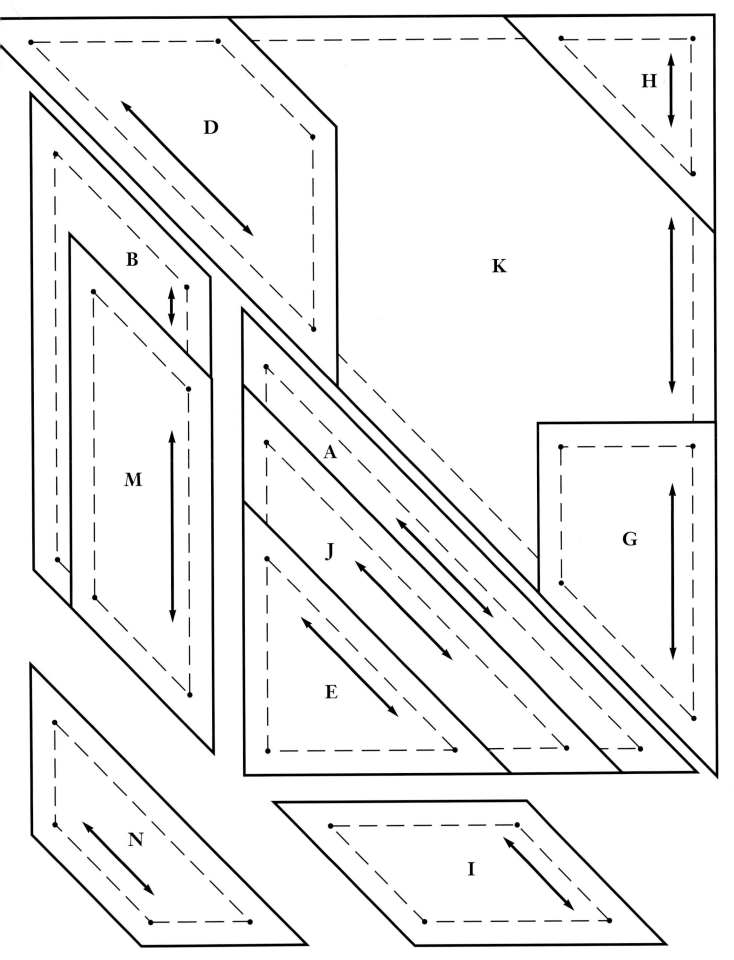

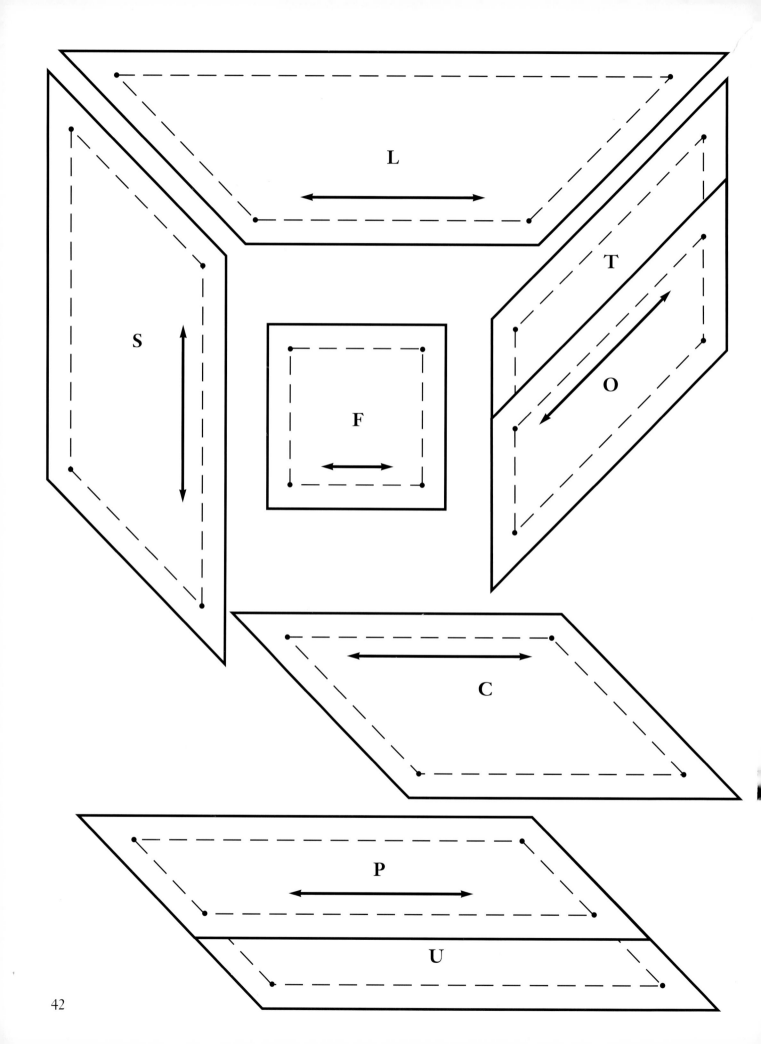

Crazy Hearts

Contrasting values of blue and white make the blocks in this little quilt seem like windows, each framing a crazy-quilt heart. The appliquéd diamonds that float between the hearts provide a calming effect, quite different from the high-energy clutter of a typical crazy quilt.

Finished Quilt Size

26" x 33½"

Number of Blocks and Finished Size

12 blocks   7½" x 7½"

Fabric Requirements

Muslin   ⅜ yard
8 blue-gray prints   scraps
White/navy
    pindot   ¾ yard
Tan-on-white
    windowpane   ⅛ yard
Blue-gray print   ¼ yard
Tan   18" square
Backing   1 yard

Other Materials

Embroidery floss   3 shades of
                                    blue gray

Number to Cut

Muslin   12 (5") squares
White/navy
    pindot   12 (8") squares
Tan-on-white
    windowpane   16 (2½") squares

Quilt Top Assembly

1. Use heart template to trace outline of heart onto center of 1 (5") muslin square. Referring to **Heart Assembly Diagram,** cover heart tracing with a variety of blue-gray print pieces, arranging shapes in a random manner. Make sure that fabric edges overlap at least ¼" and fabric extends at least ¼" beyond heart outline. Be sure to include some blue-gray scraps of the border fabric in your patch-work design.

When you are satisfied with the arrangement, turn under ¼" seam allowance on all exposed edges within heart outline and baste edges to muslin. Slipstitch folded edges to muslin. Remove basting.

Position heart template over piecing, adjusting location to make best use of fabrics. Mark outline and cut out heart piece, adding ¼" seam allowance as you cut. Repeat to make 12 hearts.

2. Turn under seam allowances on hearts. Center 1 heart on each pindot square (6 on right side of pindot and 6 on wrong side) and appliqué. Buttonhole-stitch around each heart, using 2 strands of embroidery floss **(Stitching Diagram).** Embroider lines of decorative stitching over seam lines of appliqués. Embroider additional areas within selected fabric pieces, using the design in print as a guide.

(For example, cover pindots with cross-stitches or embellish calico flowers with lazy-daisy-stitched petals and leaves.)

3. To make Row 1, join 3 heart blocks side by side in the following manner: at left, 1 block with pin-dots right side up; at center, 1 block with pindots wrong side up; at right, 1 block with pindots right side up.

Join 3 blocks for Row 2 as follows: at left, pindots wrong side up; at center, pindots right side up; at right, pindots wrong side up.

Continue to join blocks in checkerboard fashion (alternating right and wrong sides of pindot blocks) to complete rows 3 and 4.

Join rows 1–4 to complete quilt center.

4. From blue-gray print, cut 2 (2" x 28") and 2 (2" x 35½") strips. Center and join 28" strips to top and bottom edges of quilt. Center and join 35½" strips to side edges, mitering corners.

5. Turn under seam allowances on all 2½" squares and baste. Place squares on point at corners of blocks, centering each square over junction of pindot blocks **(Quilt Assembly Diagram).** Match corners of squares to seam lines of pindot blocks as shown. Appliqué squares to quilt top.

Note: Shaded heart indicates position of heart outline under fabric pieces.

Heart Assembly Diagram

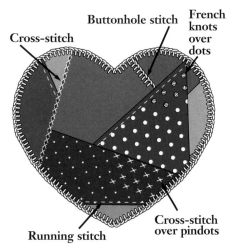

Stitching Diagram

Cross-stitch · Buttonhole stitch · French knots over dots · Running stitch · Cross-stitch over pindots

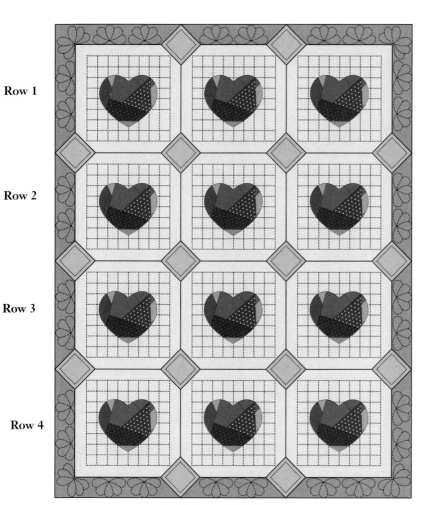

Row 1

Row 2

Row 3

Row 4

Quilt Assembly Diagram

Quilting

Mark quilting lines for blocks and diamonds, as shown in **Quilt Assembly Diagram.** Mark quilting patterns in blue border of quilt as follows: 1 corner motif in each corner and 2 border motifs between each pair of diamonds.

With white thread, quilt in-the-ditch around each block, heart, and diamond, and on all marked lines.

Finishing

Referring to instructions on page 11, make 3½ yards of 2"-wide continuous bias binding from 18" square of tan fabric. Apply binding to quilt edges.

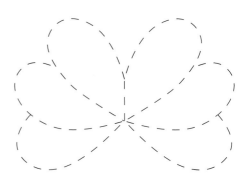

Corner Quilting Pattern

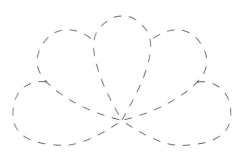

Border Quilting Pattern

Heart

Add ¼" seam allowance when cutting out hearts.

45

Hopscotch
and Butterscotch

Large pieces, geometric shapes, and quick-piecing
techniques add up to a wall hanging you can assemble in a
hop, skip, and a jump. The warm butterscotch color and
the game-board-like design works especially well in rooms
decorated with a country touch. But for a contemporary
look, simply change the colors to black, white, and red.

Finished Quilt Size

38" x 38"

Number of Blocks and Finished Size

5 Sawtooth blocks   12½" x 12½"
4 Red Square blocks 12½" x 12½"

Fabric Requirements

White   2½ yards*
Gold/white print 1 yard
Gold/dark print   ½ yard
Red pindot   ¼ yard
Backing   1⅛ yards

*Includes 18" square for bias binding.

Number to Cut

Template A	60 white
	80 gold/dark print
Template B	20 white
Template C	16 gold/dark print
Template D	16 gold/white print
Template E	16 gold/white print

Quilt Top Assembly

1. Join 4 gold/dark print As and 3 white As, as shown in **Sawtooth Strip Assembly Diagram.** Repeat to make 20 sawtooth strips.

Cut 5 (10½") squares from gold/white print. Join 1 sawtooth strip to each edge of 1 square. Add 1 white B to each corner, as shown in **Sawtooth Block Assembly Diagram.** Repeat to complete 5 Sawtooth blocks.

2. From red pindot, cut 4 (1¾" x 28") strips. From white, cut 2 (1¾" x 28") strips. Join 1 red pindot strip and 1 white strip along 1 long edge. Cut across the band to make 1¾"-wide segments **(Strip Piecing Diagram, Figure 1).** Repeat with another pair of red and white strips to make a total of 32 red/white segments. Set aside. (*Note:* To prevent raveling, seams should be stitched by machine when using this technique.)

Cut 1 (3" x 28") white strip. Join remaining red pindot strips to long edges of white strip. Cut across the band to make 16 (1¾"-wide) strips **(Figure 2).**

Join 1 gold/dark print C, 1 red/white segment, 1 gold/white print D, 1 red/white segment, and 1 gold/dark print C to make Row 1, as shown in **Red Square Block Assembly Diagram.** Repeat to make Row 5.

Join 1 red/white segment, 1 gold/white print E, 1 red/white/ red strip, 1 gold/white print E, and 1 red/white segment to make Row 2. Repeat to make Row 4.

Cut 4 (5½") squares from gold/ white print. (Join 1 gold/white print D, 1 red/white/red strip, 1 gold/white print 5½" square, 1 red/white/red strip, and 1 gold/ white print D to make Row 3.

Join rows 1–5 to make 4 Red Square blocks.

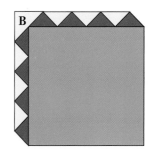

Sawtooth Strip Assembly Diagram

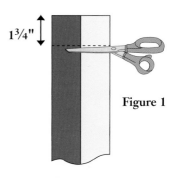

Sawtooth Block Assembly Diagram

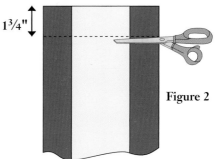

Figure 1

Figure 2

Strip Piecing Diagram

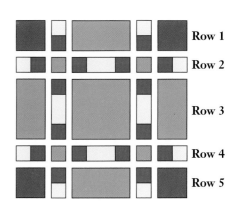

Row 1
Row 2
Row 3
Row 4
Row 5

Red Square Block Assembly Diagram

3. Join blocks to make 3 rows of 3 blocks each, as shown in **Quilt Top Assembly Diagram.** Join rows to complete quilt top.

Quilting

Mark quilting lines on quilt top, as shown in **Quilting Diagram.** Quilt on marked lines with red thread. Quilt in-the-ditch along all seams with white thread.

Finishing

Referring to instructions on page 11, make 4½ yards of 2½"-wide continuous bias binding from 18" square of white fabric. Apply binding to quilt edges.

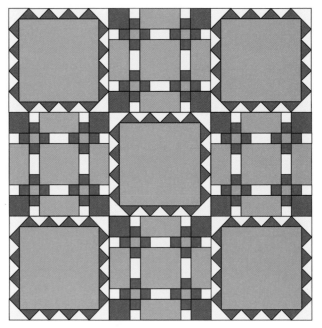

Quilt Top Assembly Diagram

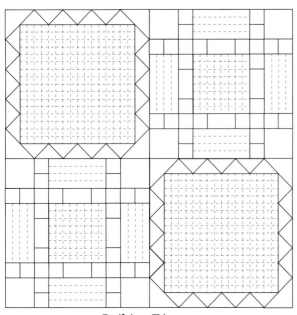

Quilting Diagram

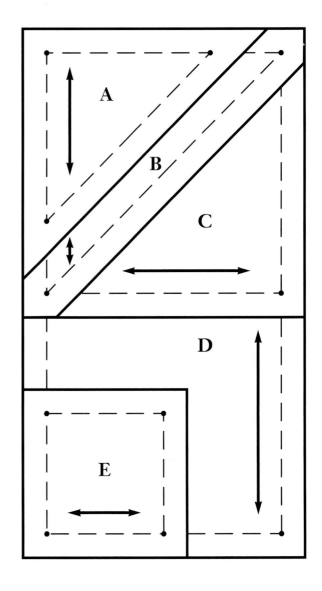